# GLASGOW

*THE PAINTINGS AND DRAWINGS OF*
*ANTHONY ARMSTRONG*

# GLASGOW

## *THE PAINTINGS AND DRAWINGS OF*

# ANTHONY ARMSTRONG

THE GLASGOW COLLECTION
IN ASSOCIATION WITH
PAUL HARRIS

First published 1990 by
The Glasgow Collection (Books)
Arrangement and edition © copyright The Glasgow Collection (Books) 1990
Pictures © copyright Anthony Armstrong 1990

*British Library Cataloguing in Publication Data*
Armstrong, Anthony *1935*–
Glasgow: the paintings and drawings of Anthony Armstrong.
1. Scottish paintings, Armstrong, Anthony 1935–
I. Title
759.2

ISBN 0-9516481-0-1

*Typeset by* Hewer Text Composition Services, Edinburgh
*Designed by* James Hutcheson *and* Paul Keir, Wide Art, Edinburgh
*Publishing Consultant* Paul Harris, Whittingehame
*Printed in* Yugoslavia *by* Gorenjski Tisk

# Acknowledgements

I should like to express my thanks to all those collectors, galleries and commercial undertakings who have graciously allowed me to reproduce works in their collections. My thanks go to The American Chemical Society, Washington DC; Cyril Gerber Fine Art Ltd, Glasgow; Gleddoch House, Langbank; The Hunterian Museum, Glasgow; the Proprietors of the Othmer Building, Washington DC; The Royal Bank of Scotland PLC; RAC Scotland; Margaret and Ralph Chidley, Alexandria, Virginia; Dr John R Donald, Glasgow; Glynis and Kenneth Heddle, Andorra; Joanna and Charles Frampton, Perthshire; Sir William Lithgow, Langbank; Sandy McCallum, Langbank; Christine and Ian McKay, Glasgow; Cecilia and William McCourt, Glasgow; Dr J McKichan, Helensburgh; Fiona and Ian Robertson, Glasgow; Pamela and Gordon Rutherford, Milngavie; R A Scott, Glasgow and Moira and Bruce Wilson, Milngavie.

Without the support and encouragement of Hamish Macfarlane and Joe Newman, Washington DC, this book would probably never have become a reality and to them my special thanks.

Finally, I owe a debt of gratitude to my family and friends for their inspiration and support, and to the Council and citizens of Glasgow.

*Anthony Armstrong*

*July 1990*

**Botanic Gardens**

# Preface

In recent years the work of Anthony Armstrong has become increasingly well known in Glasgow, the city in which he has lived for virtually all of his working life. Regular exhibition of his work has been supplemented by its reproduction in a series of prints entitled *The Glasgow Collection* and it is the availability of these limited edition prints which has taken a deeply committed artist into the homes, offices and boardrooms of the city in which he has chosen to drawn and paint over four decades.

Anthony Armstrong was born in Dundalk, Ireland, in 1935, moving to Glasgow with his mother at the age of two following the death of his father. Education at St. Aloysius School in Garnethill brought him into contact with two early and formative influences. Most important was that of the Head of Art, Donald McEvoy who was, in fact, nephew of the renowned portrait painter, Ambrose McEvoy (1878-1927), and uncle of the sculptor David McFall, born in Glasgow in 1919. McEvoy must have discerned a nascent talent for, in Tony's words, "I had the run of the place – he got me off Latin to do art!" The drawing master at the School was Gavin Alston and he also made a deep impression on the youngster. On an early *plein air* sketching expedition to Glasgow Cathedral, young Armstrong enquired of his mentor, Alston, what was to be done when the curious public gathered around, a perennial artistic problem. "That's not a problem," came the gruff reply. "Tell them to bugger off!"

It was clear that he would attend Glasgow School of Art after finishing at school. In between the two establishments of learning, Tony went to Nice on a painting holiday. "It was here that I met Matisse . . . Well, at least I saw him every morning during June of 1952 on his morning constitutional in his white suit, white hat and with his walking stick. And every day I observed to him, 'Bonjour, Monsieur Matisse!' I didn't dare take matters further!"

At Glasgow School of Art the greatest teaching influence was to be that of David Donaldson, then Head of Painting. Other students at that time – 1953-57 – included Ernest Hood, Alasdair Gray, the late Allan Fletcher, Sandy Goudie and Jimmy Robertson and amongst Tony's contemporaries were John Mathieson, Jack Knox, Anda Paterson, Norrie Kirkham and Ian McCulloch.

Quite apart from the influences of teachers and contemporaries, Tony felt himself particularly affected by the work of the Italian Primitives and the early Renaissance – in particular Masaccio (1401-28) and Piero della Francesca (ca. 1420-92). Upon this foundation of indubitable artistic integrity, was built the influences of the French Impressionists, the Glasgow School, whose work of the 1880s and early 1890s made a considerable impression, and the Post Impressionists, particularly Degas (1834-1917) and Cezanne (1839-1906).

After leaving Glasgow School of Art, Tony established himself in a studio in Queen Mary Avenue, on the south side of the City. Then there was a move to the centre into Renfrew Street, above the Clyde Automobile Company's showroom ("the Rolls Royce showroom with free heating permeating to the floor above"). The next move was more permanent and became a favourite base. At no. 77 Hill Street the studio overlooked the west wing of the School of Art (page 50) and commanded a panoramic view to the south over the River Clyde. Near here the brilliantly eccentric Alasdair Gray also had a studio. Many years later, after the demolition of the Hill Street studio, there was another move, to 14 Park Circus where, from the roof, the artist could see the Campsie Fells to the north and, to the south, the expanse of Kelvingrove Park and the sweep of the Clyde.

Enthusiasm for the subject matter of Glasgow has been balanced by the influences of travel. There has been travel to Venice, the Midi, Honolulu and, regularly, to Washington and Virginia. In addition to current studio facilities in Glasgow and Blairgowrie, Tony has a studio in Virginia at Bellhaven, between Alexandria and Mount Vernon. There have been a number of exhibitions in the United States of America in recent years and, indeed, there are many images by Armstrong of Glasgow now hanging in American homes and in public buildings in Washington DC.

The influence of Edgar Degas seems to be apparent in a predilection for pastel painting. Some of Tony's strongest work is in pastel, as is evidenced by the success of the Glasgow Collection prints. Pastel sketches are made by applying the basic colour materials with the fingers – "direct expression of the visual through the hands without an implement". The pastel studies are characterised by the use of rich colours, by subtle blending and careful suggestion: a sort of conjunction of Armstrong, Degas and ancient cave painting.

Pen sketches are produced in vast numbers; direct drawing with no corrections or rubbing out. "A flow of visual ideas with no second thoughts." In the streets, in the bars, in workplaces the notebook is out and the pen is busy.

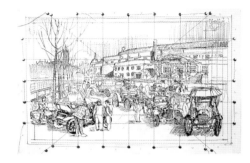

Oil is less commonly used. Its special qualities appear to be reserved for larger scale works. "So often the nature of the concept itself dictates the choice of medium. Oil has the advantage that, in complex situations, it can be worked on over an extended period of time." The painting executed for the Royal Automobile Club for presentation to the Museum of Transport (pages 70-1) is a case in point.

Ideas are jotted into sketchbooks. Details are noted. Sometimes quick colour studies are made. Loose drawings, loose colour studies, tight and detailed drawings are combined together and worked up in a method also used by Turner. Drawings and studies are transferred to larger and more ambitious formats by enlarging onto a grid and tracing. The oils are often built up over a period of time, a year being quite common. Very often unfinished or apparently abandoned works are taken up again later.

As a man, Anthony Armstrong is no reclusive garret dweller, furtively emerging to make his sketches before retiring for some extended, manic painting session. Indeed, his work reflects his wide interests and participation in what might be regarded, especially by him, as the more mind expanding activities of man and which often serve to lend a certain frisson to his work: eating, drinking, good company, vintage and classic motor cars and the appreciation of fine buildings are all writ large in his work. Based upon solid credentials, it combines traditional artistic values with a very real flair for capturing that moment in time: the glance across a bar, the juxtaposition of 'the wee Glesga mannie' and the architecture of the Victorian city, the things that were and are no more. With the opportunity for wide travel and exhibition abroad, he has actively chosen the City of Glasgow to feature predominantly in his sketchbook and on his palette. In years to come, it is not unreasonable to suppose, his work will form a unique record of the City during a period of vital transition. There is no trace of pretension about Tony's *oeuvre*. In the case of Anthony Armstrong there can be no doubt that the paintings *are* the man.

*Paul Harris*

George Sq. Aug 90

# Contents

# GLASGOW

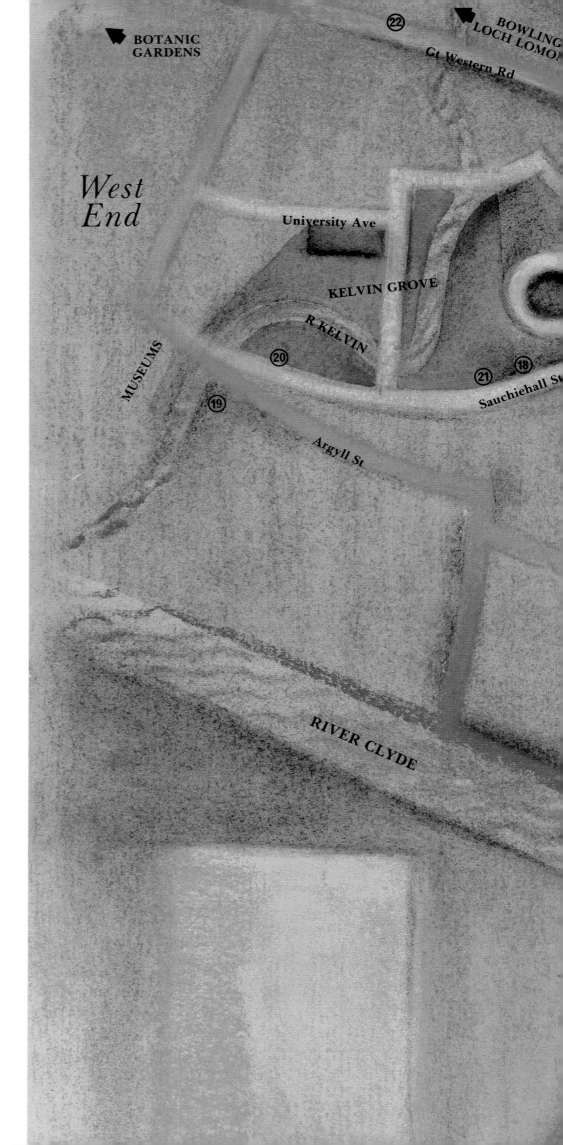

St George's Cross

Maryhill Rd

Edinburgh ➤

M8    Motorway

Cowcaddens

① 

⑭

CHARING
CROSS

Sauchiehall St

Castle St

CATHEDRAL

⑮

⑬          Bath Street

⑯   ⑰

CITY
ST
STATION

West George St

Elm Bank St

Hope St

⑫

George
Square

East
End

Ingram St

High St

MERCHANT
CITY

⑧

Union St

⑨     ⑪

Argyll St

Broomielaw

⑦

CENTRAL
STATION

Trongate

GLASGOW
CROSS

⑩

Briggait

St Andrews Sq

② 

⑤           ④

POLLOCK HOUSE & PARK
THE BURRELL COLLECTION

RIVER CLYDE

③

GLASGOW GREEN

⑥

Southside

# *The Old City*

"And now what *am* I to say of this Glasgow, which is at once a city of the greatest beauty, a commercial town, and a place of manufactures also very great?

"The whole is built of beautiful white stone; and doors, windows, and everything, bespeak solid worth, without any taste for ostentation or show."

William Cobbett *Cobbett's Tour in Scotland* (1833)

The 13th century Cathedral of St Mungo, or Kentigern, lies at the very heart of the old town, the 'dear green place' of the Gaelic which is sometimes believed to have lent its name to the old expanding city of Glasgow. On the sloping banks of the Molendinar Burn the columns and vaults of the great Church were erected, the 'low-browed, dark and twilight vaults' of Scott in Rob Roy. Just as Charles Rennie Mackintosh painted one of his earliest known watercolours of the Cathedral, so Anthony Armstrong, as a young schoolboy in the early 1950s, chose this as his first subject for a painting *en plein air*.

**Glasgow Cathedral**

16

**Provand's Lordship**

This view of the ancient Cathedral precinct has now been obscured by recent redevelopment.

**Cathedral Precinct**

The ancient three-storey manse of Provand's Lordship, believed to be the oldest house in Glasgow, was built in the late 15th century and is an impressive relic of mediaeval life.

The positively rural charms of the Cathedral precincts were described by Harriet Beecher Stowe in 1854:

"This was my first experience in cathedrals. It was a new thing to me altogether, and as I walked along under the old buttresses and battlements without, and looked into the bewildering labyrinths of architecture within, I saw that, with silence and solitude to help the impression, the old building might become a strong part of one's inner life. A grave-yard crowded with flat stones lies all around it. A deep ravine separates it from another cemetery on an opposite eminence, rustling with dark pines. A little brook murmurs with its slender voice between."

Harriet Beecher Stowe *Sunny Memories of Foreign Lands* (1854)

**Provand's Lordship**

**Fountain, Glasgow Green**

"By the side of the river, above the bridges, there is a place modestly called Glasgow Green, containing about a hundred English acres of land, which is in very fine green sward, and is at all times open for the citizens to go for their recreation."

William Cobbett *Cobbett's Tour in Scotland* (1833)

Glasgow Green is the great green open space in the City which has seen so much of the life of Glasgow over the centuries. The neo-classical Greek style High Court building of the early 19th century is a building of austere and simple elegance with its vast portico and indisputable dignity. The 46-foot high Fountain was manufactured in terracotta and formed the main Doulton exhibit at the 1888 International Exhibition at Kelvingrove. Presented to the City by Sir Henry Doulton, it was re-erected on the Green. Alas, the great Fountain is no longer in operation and this potentially stunning artefact has lain for many years in a state of rapidly increasing decay.

Glasgow Green

The great Triumphal Arch, designed by James Adam in 1796 was removed painstakingly, stone by stone, from the demolished Athenaeum in Ingram Street and rebuilt on the Green.

**Triumphal Arch, Glasgow Green**

One of Glasgow's most stunning buildings, the polychromatic brick-built palazzo which used to be Templeton's Carpet Factory. It was designed by William Leiper (1889) and extended in the 1930s. It now houses the Templeton Business Centre.

**Working drawings: Templeton's & Triumphal Arch and School**

**Templeton's Carpet Factory**

The People's Palace, built in 1894, sits upon Glasgow Green, the Winter Gardens appended to the back. The Nelson Obelisk, designed by David Hamilton in 1806, erected, and almost immmediately struck by lightning.

**Working drawings: Interior of Winter Garden, The Peoples' Palace and Obelisk**

**Study: Paddy's Market**

In Paddy's Market is all the hustle and the bustle of street markets since time immemorial. A favourite subject for Armstrong, he was much influenced to capture this subject by the earlier engravings and drawings of artists like Piranesi.

**Paddy's Market**

Armstrong 12.46    Thu. 1.30.
                   noon 3rd Nov 88

**Paddy's Market with railway arch**

**Old Merchant House Tower**

33

**Study: Frontage of old Fishmarket**

The Briggait was built originally as the Fishmarket and encompasses a vast hall with cast iron galleries. Although beautifully restored in recent years and put into use as as a shopping centre, it was not destined to enjoy commercial success and now lies virtually abandoned despite its potential as a maritime and river museum.

**The Briggait**

**Glasgow Cross, Holiday Monday**

**The Trongate**

**St. Andrew Street**

The baroque, generously proportioned St Andrew's Kirk, built between 1739 and 1759, was, at the time, regarded as the finest church of its day. The enormous portico occasioned such alarm amongst the populace that the mason, Nasmith, felt obliged to sleep beneath it the first night after the removal of the temporary centre supports.

**St. Andrew Kirk**

# The Second City

Although it is difficult to envisage today, George Square was originally a large, quiet classical square of three storey houses with a private fenced garden in the middle. The architects Robert and James Adam started work on it in 1786 but, failing to win commercial success, it was soon invaded by hotels and business premises, encouraged by the development of the railway terminus. By the middle of the century, there was not a private house in occupation and municipally-inspired monuments had taken over the gardens.

William Young's grandiose edifice that was to be the City Chambers took shape in the 1880s and one of the most interesting, and uniquely Glasgow, features in this Venetian influenced extravaganza remains the magnificent Banqueting Hall with mural decorations by the Glasgow Boys, including Lavery, Walton, Roche and Henry. In the foreground, is the corner of the Merchants' House by John Burnet (1874-7).

**The Clyde Port Authority Building**

**George Square with Merchant's House (foreground)**

Hutcheson's Hospital and Old Sheriff Court

The Trades House, Glassford St

**Candleriggs**

Hutcheson's Hospital was founded in 1639, by lawyers George and Thomas Hutcheson of Lambhill, for 12 old men and 12 boys. The new building in Ingram Street replaced the old, which faced onto the Trongate, in 1802, an early work of up and coming architect David Hamilton. The Old Sheriff Court building of 1844 has now abandoned its judiciary role and is the subject of plans for conversion into a fashion centre.

The Old Fruitmarket was housed in the Victorian galleried market hall fronting onto the Bell Street side of the City Hall.

After the great fire of 1677, the candlemakers of the city were relocated and the Candleriggs was opened up as the route to the north with the Ramshorn Kirk, completed in 1724, at its head. The City Hall took over as the city's concert venue from St Andrew's Halls following their destruction by fire. The adjacent building was formerly the bustling fruit market with copious use of cast iron and vast galleried hall.

Old Fruit Market.

43

**West George Street**

West George Street was originally known as Camperdown Place –
after the great naval victory and was so named to partner St Vincent
Place to the south. Evidence of the fine terraced houses built shortly
after 1800 has now virtually disappeared, at least in that section
nearest town and but one town house now remains. On the left is the
tall, narrow Hatrack Building built in 1899 in *art nouveau* style.

**Theatre Royal Rehearsal Rooms**

**Old Glasgow High School**

From plinths over the entrance portico of the old Glasgow High School building the stone-sculpted figures of Homer, Cicero, Galileo and James Watt look down onto Elmbank Street. Immediately behind the old High School, work is going on the construction of the Britoil building.

The King's Theatre, pictured here from Bath Street, was designed by Frank Matcham in 1904 and built in red sandstone. The proximity of the inner ring road developments of the 1960s has meant that most of the great 19th century buildings of Elmbank Street have now disappeared. One small terrace and the King's Theatre are all that remains.

**King's Theatre from Bath Street**

*12 nom 6ª March 88.    II Theatre Roy*

**STV Studios, Cowcaddens**

The Theatre Royal, formerly the Royal Colosseum (1867), a low music hall, entered by way of an arcade from Cowcaddens. Behind the undistinguished facade lurks a wonderful interior with its auditorium by C J Phipps (1895). In the 1950s it was converted to house the offices and studios of STV and passed by them to Scottish Opera in 1975. A new foyer was built to the designs of Derek Sugden and STV rehoused itself in the modern block at the back of the theatre.

**Theatre Royal, Hope Street**

**Redevelopment Sauchiehall Street**

**Colour study: Reid & Todd building**

**The Artists Studio, Garnethill**

From 1953 to 1957 Armstrong was a student at Glasgow School of Art and had a studio nearby in Hill Street from which he could draw the cityscape and the School. His friend and fellow student Alasdair Gray also had his studio in Hill Street. This studio was used for many years after he left the School of Art but as redevelopment encroached upon the street the 'artists' colony' known as the Latin Quarter was forced out.

Glasgow School of Art is indubitably Charles Rennie Mackintosh's masterwork. The commission was won in competition by the then young Mackintosh. His presentation benefited from his close relationship with his mentor Fra Newbery but the latter did take a considerable risk in backing his favourite, former pupil.

**Early drawing of west wing, Glasgow School of Art**

**Glasgow School of Art from Bath St**

**Composition**

**Library Wing, Glasgow School of Art**

**Motorway Fly-over, Charing Cross**

**Mitchell Library**

The Italian Renaissance style Queen's Rooms in the lyrically named La Belle Place were built in the 1850s to accommodate a whole suite of assembly rooms and a concert hall designed to meet the needs of a new community formed by the spread westwards.

The Mitchell Library built between 1906 and 1911 is a fitting repository for so much of the city's research and reading materials. Its vast Renaissance style bulk seemingly refuses to be intimidated by the motorway buzzing at its feet whilst inside its marble staircases and polished wood interiors are redolent of an age with considerably more gravitas.

The French-influenced Charing Cross Mansions, designed by Burnet, Son & Campbell, 1889-9, is an enduring reminder of a somewhat heavy grandeur that was late Victorian Glasgow. It was dubbed 'The Mairie of the Charing Cross arondissement' by Sir John Summerson. It survived the motorways driven through the city but yards away.

**La Belle Place**

**Charing Cross**

**Royal Crescent**

# The West End

**Glasgow Univerity – Old and New**

The University moved to Gilmorehill in 1868. Building started in 1867 on Sir George Gilbert Scott's magnificent Gothic Revival building and the Prince of Wales laid the foundation stone in October of the following year. The *Glasgow Herald* reporter on the scene on entering the quadrangle of the College "was amazed by the circular sea of faces which burst upon my sight in a moment. The whole space, in fact, was packed with human beings, to the number, it is said, of 20,000, all in holiday attire; while the tops of the walls, the scaffold poles, the trees inside, and even the building cranes, were crowded as thickly as men and boys could sit or stand."

At the opening of the University buildings at Gilmorehill in 1868, Kelvingrove Park was seen at its busiest ever by the *Glasgow Herald* reporter: "I looked towards the West End Park and the prospect was magnificent. People were dotted over its whole surface, and in some parts they were packed as thickly as they could stand, while from the top of Gilmorehill to the eastern end of the Park there stretched the long serpentine double line of Volunteers, on the route to be taken by the returning carriages."

**Park Circus Garden with University Tower**

**Park Circus: Tree**

**Kelvingrove**

*Serenata* to the West End Park

It's long pest midnight, there's
    no one in the street,
The consteble is sleeping at the
    corner of his beat.
The cold white erc-lamps fizz
    like gingerade,
And I'm below your window
    with this cherming serenade.
Open your window the nicht is
    beastly dark,
The phantoms are dencing in
    the West-End Park,
Open your window, your lover
    brave to see,
I'm here all alone, and there's
no-one here but me!

        James Bridie

**Panorama, Kelvingrove**

**Entrance to Park from Argyle Street**

"Our first gathering in our splendid Art Galleries, inaugurated only yesterday by the King's eldest daughter, must needs be a memorable one. The long corridors, in a blaze of light, the great halls of statuary were to be seen under the happiest of auspices, with music playing and a gay crowd of citizens in uniform and brightly coloured gowns moving among the palms and statues and making the scene brilliant and picturesque. The walls were, it must be confessed, only of interest to the passing eye, and the treasures they displayed were for the time being only glanced at casually with good intentions of learning to know them another day. The scene from the windows that looked on the lively grounds of the Exhibition was for the moment more to our taste . . .".

*Evening News*, May 3 1901

Kelvingrove Art Gallery and Museum had its genesis in the first great Glasgow Exhibition of 1888. An enormous success, the profits were allocated to a new Art Gallery and Museum and there was an open architectural competition in 1891. The enormous red sandstone, Renaissance style building was opened just in time for the 1901 Exhibition. Popular legend has it to this day that the Gallery was built back to front and that the poor architect perforce jumped from the tower . . .

**Museum and Art Gallery**

Armstrong

**The Old Gatehouse at the University**

The Old Gatehouse at the University had been removed stone by stone from the High Street and was rebuilt in University Avenue.

**University from Kelvin Way**

**Argyle Street**

**The Haugh**

The painting in oil by Anthony Armstrong commissioned by the Royal Automobile Club and donated to the new Museum of Transport, located in Kelvin Hall, April 1990.

**Preparing for the Rally**

**Argyll 1913**

**Argyll Motor Car, 1907**

Working drawings and studies of vintage cars and figures which were made for the RAC commission. Vintage and classic cars have been a lifelong interest for the artist.

**Arrol-Johnston Motor Car, 1905**

**Arrol-Johnston Motor Car, 1901**

Glasgow Academy of 1878, described by one modern critic as a "Germanic institutional block" with Belmont Church in the background.

Great Western Road is to this day "one of the longest, straightest, and most elegant streets in Glasgow" (C. Kirkwood: The Dictionary of Glasgow, 1884). In this pastel, we see, on the right, the Cooper Building and, beyond Kelvin Bridge, St. Mary's Cathedral and Lynedoch Church.

**Glasgow Academy with Belmont Church beyond**

**Great Western Road**

**North Range, Botanic Gardens, with BBC Studios Beyond**

**The Fish Pond, Botanic Gardens**

The Botanic Gardens were first opened in 1842. The quite extraordinary glass structure in the picture was bought from John Kibble in Colport in 1871 and re-erected in the Botanic Gardens. Under the arrangement reached with the Directors, Kibble retained free use of the building, as required, for 21 years and it became the social centre for the West end of Glasgow with its concerts, parties and entertainments. On summer evenings it was packed with the loud and the louche who brought about such a trail of damage that the authorities felt obliged to buy out Kibble's lease and they ultimately went bankrupt in 1887. After this, the Botanics were taken over by the City Corporation who made a series of improvements, including the addition of the entrance aisle with its glass covered transept.

People in the Park

Sunbathers

**The Burrell Collection**

**Pollok House**

# Going out of Town

Upon Strathmore.

**Pinxton Tower from Cowcaddens, 1972**

The line of Maryhill Road into the City marks the route of the old cattle drovers, whose long and arduous journey ended at Cowcaddens, where the cattle came down into the city.

The former village of Maryhill became integrated into the City but was a quite different place in the middle of the 19th century:

"The village of Maryhill is in the immediate vicinity of the bridge, from which it is seen in its most favourable aspect. Being nearly if not altogether of modern erection, the village has a clean and tidy appearance, and is arranged with considerable regularity. There is a number of public works, such as printfields and establishments for bleaching, in its vicinity, in which the population (a large proportion of whom are of Irish origin) are principally employed. The village itself presents few attractions to the rambler, but the country in its neighbourhood, especially along the valley of the Kelvin, is characterised by a more than ordinary degree of beauty."

Hugh Macdonald *Rambles Round Glasgow* (1854)

**Maryhill Road with church**

**The Black Tenement**

**Cooperage Interior**

Draw thy fierce streams of blinding ore,
Smite on thy thousands anvil, roar
    Down to the harbour bars;
Smoulder in smoky sunsets, flare
On rainy nights, when street and square
    Lie empty to the stars.
From terrace proud to alley base
I know thee as my mother's face.
        from Alexander Smith (1830-67) *Glasgow*

**Study for Cooperage Painting**

**Barrel Slats**

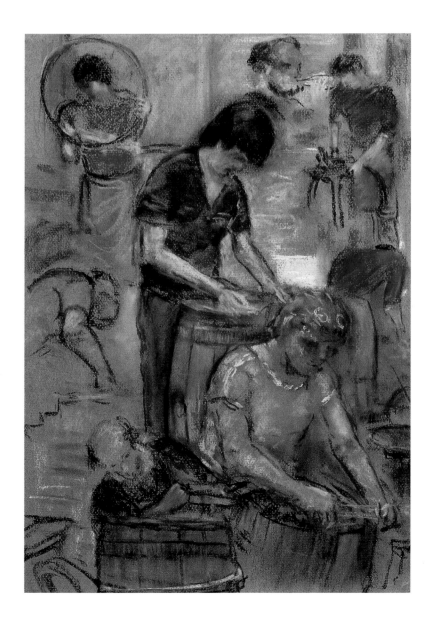

**Production Processes at the Cooperage**

**The Butnay**

The 'Butnay'. It was from here that discomfited Glaswegians and West Highlanders took ship to Australia: to Botany Bay, lending the one time embarkation point for Bowling its curious name.

**Aqueduct, Canal at Maryhill**

**Pinxton**

**The *Vital Spark* at Bowling**

**Bowling**

The puffer *The Vital Spark* was laid up at Bowling after her starring role in the televised version of Neil Munro's classic tales of West coast nautical chicanery and ineptitude. Once a centre for shipbuilding and distilling, Bowling now boasts the somewhat more modern attributes of leisure park and marina.

**Bird Sanctuary**

**Flooding near Balmaha**

The Queen's View towards Loch Lomond

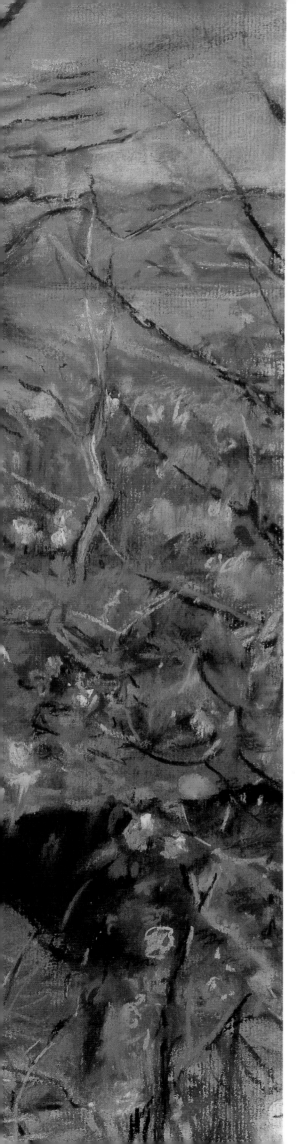

Loch Lomond has been a traditional weekend and holiday playground for generations of Glaswegians.

"Loch Lomond lies quite near to Glasgow. Nice Glaswegians motor out there and admire the scenery and calculate its horse-power and drink whisky and chaff one another in genteelly Anglicised Glaswegianisms. After a hasty look at Glasgow the investigator would do well to disguise himself as one of like kind, drive down to Loch Lomondside and stare across its waters at the sailing clouds that crown the Ben, at the flooding of colours changing and darkling and miraculously lighting up and down those misty slopes . . . This is the proper land and stance from which to look at Glasgow . . ."

Lewis Grassic Gibbon *Scottish Scene*

**Cattle by the Burn near Loch Lomond**

By yon bonnie banks, and by yon bonnie braes,
Where the sun shines bright on Loch Lomond;
Where me and my true love where ever wont to gae,
On the bonnie, bonnie banks o' Loch Lomond.

And you'll take' the high road and I'll tak' the low road,
And I'll be in Scotland afore ye;
But me and my true love will never meet again
On the bonnie, bonnie banks o' Loch Lomond

Traditional air

**Flooding near Balmaha**

**Berrypicking, Blairgowrie**

At the berrypicking, Blairgowrie. For many Glaswegians, the berrypicking was a welcome opportunity for a couple of weeks of paid holiday in the fresh air of Angus or Perthshire.

The Berryfields o' Blair

There's corner boys fae Glesca
Kettle boilers fae Lochee,
Miners fae the pits o' Fife
Millworkers fae Dundee. There's fisher folk fae Peterhead
And tramps fae everywhere,
A' lookin' for a livin'
Aff the berryfields o' Blair

Belle Stewart

**Children at the Berrypicking**

**Fruit Farm, Blairgowrie**

**Tea Break**

# Doon the Watter

**Shingle Beach with Carousel, Largs**

Largs looking North

Largs looking South

Pride of the Clyde: The paddlesteamer *Waverley*. Redolent of a romanticised bygone age of trips 'doon the watter'.

The writer J J Bell captured the essence of 'doon the watter':

"The Glasgow summer holiday was then essentially a family affair. Even when the children were grown up, they did not go their different ways. I remember a family of thirteen holidaying together. . . the usual method for families like ours was to 'sail all the way', either from the Broomielaw or Partick Pier.

"We arrived at Partick Pier far too early. The sun shone hotly; the tide was low; and it was before the days of the Clyde's purification. Not to be squeamish about it, the Clyde at Glasgow was then a big sewer. We and other families waited and waited. In the heat babies began to 'girn'; small children grew peevish; little girls complained or looked pathetically patient. For boys there was always the entertainment of the shipping – liners, channnel and river steamers, cargo vessels, barques, barquentines, brigs and schooners, dredgers, hoppers, ferries."

J J Bell *I Remember* (1932)

**The Paddle Steamer *Waverley* on the Clyde**

Noon Looking West.    Millgate

"She came alongside; the families were shepherded on board, to find seats where they could, and the luggage was added to the existing mountains. Luggage went free then. Years later, I witnessed the indignation of a family at being charged a trifle for their piano's conveyance. The *Benmore* resumed her journey, still cannily, for every now and then appeared on the banks boards bearing the words 'Dead Slow', the warning necessary in order that the wash from steamers should break lightly against the shores of the shipyards or the dredgers at work."

J J Bell *I Remember* (1932)

**The Wee Cumbrae from Millport**

Ponies on the Beach

Millport. July. 3p..

"But I never saw bathing performed by ladies in Scotland even with common decency. Why the devil can't they use bathing machines, or go into retired places? There was one bathing machine on the beach at Ardrossan, which was rarely used, and two in the inn court, which the landlord told me were never used at all."

Henry Cockburn *Circuit Journeys* (1888)

**Figure studies: On the Beach**

**Fintray Bay**

"The public, however, having gained confidence by degrees, in a navigation which became at once expeditious and pleasant, it was preferrred to every other mode of conveyance; for the expedition of the voyage, and beauty of the scenery on the banks of the Clyde, are such as to attract alike the attention of the man of business and pleasure; and the watering places all along the coast have been crowded with company beyond all former precedent, in consequence of steam conveyance . . . Since the *Comet* began to ply on the River, it is very common to make the voyage of Campbeltown, Inverary, or the Kyles of Bute, and return to Glasgow on the following day."

James Cleland *Annals of Glasgow* (1816)

**Shivering**

**Yachting on the Clyde**

**Detail, The Maiden Rocks**

Arran

Here, as of old, the dreaming hours fulfil
Their ancient pledge, and flower in sunlit days
Above thy pastoral slopes and wave-washed bays
Where melody and colour merge and thrill.
Thy chosen Priestess, Beauty, beckons still
From whin-clad straths and heather-haunted ways,
Or lies in wait along the scented braes,
Or chains a leafy thought from hill to hill.

Bruce found a shelter, lovely Isle, in thee
When o'er his head the cloud of menace rolled,
He saw thy rock-strewn mountains tipped with gold
When morn rose sovran from the murmuring sea,
And on thy bosom, fold on mistly fold,
Beheld her dew-stained garments floating free.

Ferdinand E Kappey

**The Maidens with the Hills of Arran beyond**

**Sketch: On the Clyde Coast**

**Family**

# Back in Town

**Conversation**

**Contre-jour**

De Quincey's is on the site where the English opium eater Thomas de Quincey lived in Glasgow during the 1840s. Restored and converted into an eatery, the interior is renowned for its tile-work, uncovered during conversion work.

De Quincey's

**Conversation**

**Nico's II**

**The Long Bar**

Interior of Nico's. One of the many chic eateries which grew up in
Glasgow in the '70s and '80s.

**The Three Friends**

The guests are met, the feast is set.

Samuel Taylor Coleridge *The Ancient Mariner*

Tell me not in figures wavy
    That my bill is twelve-and-nine
When I had but soup of gravy,
    Steak, potatoes, cheese, and wine.
Adrian Ross *The Salmi of Life*

There is no love sincerer than the love of food.
George Bernard Shaw

At the Bar

**Girl with Red Hair**

122

**Glasgow Girls**

**The Little Artist**

**Mother and Child**

**Red-haired Boy**

**Boy Drawing**

**Two Friends**

**Brasserie**

To Youth
Drink wine, and live here blithefull, while ye may:
The morrowes life too late is, live today.
                    Robert Herrick


A Bottle and a Friend

Here's a bottle and an honest friend
    What wad ye wish for mair, man?
Wha kens, before his life may end,
    What his share may be o'care, man?
                    Robert Burns (1759-96)

**Nico's**

**Study of an Entertainer**

**Evening Encounter**

The Student

**Early pastel ca. 1960: Glasgow Cross**

Above Queen St. . 18th Aug 90